Holland's Big Red
My Happy Place

Kimberly M. Johnson

WestBow Press books may be ordered through booksellers or by contacting:

WestBow Press
A Division of Thomas Nelson & Zondervan
1663 Liberty Drive
Bloomington, IN 47403
www.westbowpress.com
844-714-3454

Scripture quotations are from The ESV® Bible (The Holy Bible, English Standard Version®), copyright © 2001 by Crossway, a publishing ministry of Good News Publishers. Used by permission. All rights reserved.

ISBN: 978-1-6642-3747-6 (sc)
ISBN: 978-1-6642-3748-3 (e)

Library of Congress Control Number: 2021912228

Print information available on the last page.

WestBow Press rev. date: 10/15/2021

WESTBOW
PRESS®
A DIVISION OF THOMAS NELSON
& ZONDERVAN

Holland's Big Red
My Happy Place

Kimberly M. Johnson

For my mom, Georgia Mae Johnson

You were my biggest cheerleader, encourager, and support. I love you and wish you were here to celebrate this book with me.

For my third grade teacher and friend. Annette Witham
Thank you for helping edit this book with me it has been an honor.
But most of all thank you for being my third grade teacher and now my friend.

Mom, my sister Nina and I headed out to Holland State Park. We planned to take one last visit to my favorite spot, Big Red.

It's my happy place.

I was so excited to be able to see Big Red one last time on this beautiful day.

It was the Saturday after Labor Day. For many, the summer season was over. But it didn't look over today, not in West Michigan.

The day was clear and
beautiful with perfect
weather at seventy-eight
degrees.

Boats were going through
the Holland Channel.
For many it would be their
last time for this year.

A quick but hearty wave comes from ship to shore.

It's a beautiful day, now isn't it?" The man shouts from his boat.

Sailboats are my favorite.

The waves crashed as we watch from the pier. Nina says she saw a fish jump, she is sure it was a steelhead.

The last time to lay in the warm sun.

Paddle boarders and swimmers enjoy the water and warm temperature.

Sometimes I like to just sit quietly and enjoy Big Red.

Sometimes Nina joins me. I don't mind as long as she is quiet and doesn't ask a lot of questions.

You know how sisters can be.

Crashing waves!

Splashing waves in beautiful Lake Michigan!

One last splash along the lakeshore.

Foot prints I make in the sand as I take a short walk along the shore to get a closer look at Big Red.

And like our warm weather soon will be,
my footprints are gone.

Pretty soon mom said that it would be getting dark, and that we needed to start packing up and heading home.

In September, the sun goes down sooner and more quickly than in the summer months.

So I only had a few more minutes.

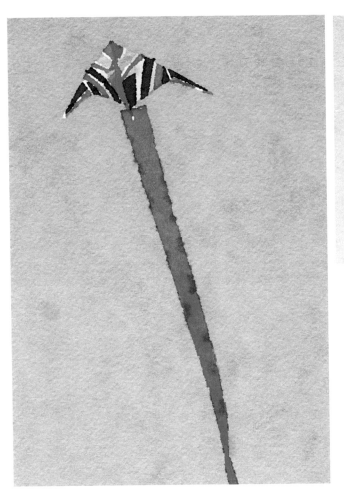

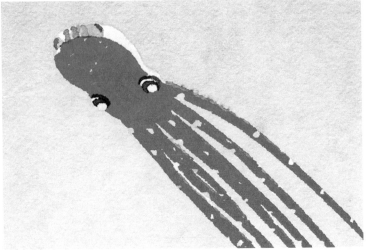

I saw two kites for the last time this season.

Sailboats coming in for the evening.

I looked up and the sun was going down.

The sun was getting lower and lower.

And just like that.

The sun was gone.

One last twilight with Big Red. It makes me kind of sad.

Well Big Red, I have to go now. Thank you for making this my happy place.

Have a great winter, I am really going to miss you. See you next summer.

Just then, the lights came on.
It was as if Big Red was answering,
"Sure thing, I will wait here for you."

"Good night, Big Red"

Then I slept all the way back home.

Kimberly Johnson
is a local artist from West Michigan. She has been drawing since she was a small child, when her mother would bring home scrap paper from work to draw on. On that scrap paper she would write and illustrate stories for her mother and teachers. She has exhibited her work in ten years of Art Prize, as well as other galleries around the city including a permanent exhibit at a Mercy Health clinic in Southeast Grand Rapids.

She also has taught Preschool in the Grand Rapids area.

Printed in the United States
by Baker & Taylor Publisher Services